I0468816

Table of Contents

whatsoever on the behalf of the purchaser or reader of these materials. Any perceived slight of any individual or organization is purely unintentional. I sometimes use affiliate links in the content. This means if you decide to make a purchase, I will get a sales commission. But that doesn't mean my opinion is for sale. Every affiliate link on is to products that I've personally used and found useful. Please do your own research before making any purchase online.

Printed in the United States of America

First Printing, 2016

ISBN-13: 978-1523880782

www.richardallenwilliamsjr.com

info@richardallenwilliamsjr.com

~ ACKNOWLEDGEMENTS~

~FIRST OF ALL I WANT TO GIVE HONOR TO GOD FOR THIS PRIVILGE. I THANK FOR HIS LOVE, GUIDANCE, AND ENCOURAGEMENT. I AM GRATEFUL FOR THIS OPPORTUNITY TO SHARE WITH THE WORLD WHAT I HAVE LEARN. THIS IS MY FIRST BOOK AND I WANT TO DEDICATED THIS TO MY GRANDPAPA" JAMES A. FINNEY" WHO TOLD ME I COULD DO ANYTHING, I MISS YOU AND THANK YOU FOR THE LESSONS YOU TAUGHT ME. TO MY MOM, DAD, ALONI, KARYLN-I LOVE YOU ALL. I AM TRULY BLESSED YOU GUYS ALWAYS SUPPORT ME NO MATTER WHAT I DO- THANK YOU. I ALSO WANT SAY A SPECIAL THANKS TO MY ANGEL KRYSSHONDA ITS BEEN ONLY FIVE YEARS BUT IT FEELS LIKE WE'VE BEEN TOGETHER FOREVER. BUT NOT ONE DAY GOES BY THAT I'M NOT IN AWE OF YOU. THANK YOU SO PUSHING ME, PRESSING ME AND LOVING ME. TO OUR FIVE HANDSOME BOYS: JOSIAH, ELIJAH, BRITTAIN, RICHARD, AND ZACHIACH THANK FOR BEING SOME THE MOST WONDERFUL SONS A FATHER COULD ASK FOR CHEERING ME I LOVE YOU GUY THIS IS FOR YOU. ~

INTRODUCTION

How to build a successful sale's funnel: Email Marketing Released? Having a "successful sale's funnel" seems like the perfect dream for any business. You have a bottom line that keeps bringing in profits. With open rates which are through the roof allowing you to be able to sit back and sip margaritas watching the money come rolling in.

But reality, however, is much more different than this dream. Building a successful sale's funnel for your business is about establishing a responsive list that looks forward to receiving your emails, because of the value your company adds their lives. Whether through your products or services they have come to trust and love your brand and can't wait to see what's next.

Companies like Google, Amazon, Airing, E-bay and Apple understand it's all about staying connected with your customer's likes and dislikes to help you to create products and services they come to love. What is the easiest way to turning your potential customers from strangers to friends then through a platform such as email marketing that allows you to be more personal with client base? This is a critical part of your business which will help you to be more, laser-focused with your offers allowing you to propel your company to the next level.

It doesn't matter if you're a new start up, author, affiliate marketer, or a "veteran" Internet entrepreneur. Anyone who wants to build a successful sale's funnel needs to work at building a strong email list that gets things done. That way you'll have more time to focus on creating products and offers that your customers will fall in love with. You have a unique challenge as an entrepreneur, business owner, author or an Internet marketer. Being a 'solopreneur' is a scary thought to some.

But it's also comforting because it means you have the ability to determine your own business future. Ultimately the income you generate will be directly related to how you manage the marketing and promotion of your company. Ask yourself are you making your bottom line a priority? Or are you just wishing more people will eventually learn about you and your company but doing nothing to make them aware? Do you believe that somehow that will increase your sales and skyrocket your revenue?

Let say this if you are reading this book and don't have email list and never thought about getting one established then sadly you have miss the boat. Because this missing part of your sale's funnel could leave you spinning your wheels while other businesses move ahead? Every single day you have a choice, but let me assure you if you are reading this book have already made the choice. You have already made a decision to work on the important parts of your business whether you know it or not. That's why I wrote How to build a successful sale's: Email

Marketing Strategies Released. What you'll find here is a step-by-step system for running an email marketing campaign that will help you have a super successful business.

Unlike other email marketing books you'll get a blueprint that is specifically written for anyone looking to make their company a success. My goal isn't to tell you what to do and you have figure out how to get everything set up yourself. Where's the fun in that? Instead I'm going to detail a proven strategy for focusing on the important things when it comes to your email marketing strategy and getting results from your email list.

Who Am I? You might wonder what makes me an expert on email marketing. So let me introduce myself… My name is Richard Williams Jr.

I have been a full-time Internet entrepreneur since 2010. I've run a variety of businesses like: Affiliate marketing, blogging, Web Hosting, Web design, and info product creation. I've had my hand in a lot of pies. More importantly, I've learned what works (and doesn't work) with Email Marketing. More importantly, I'm an advocate of small businesses.

So you only need to worry about a few things to run a profitable email marketing campaign. Concentrate on these critical factors and you can achieve success without working yourself into the ground trying to find out an easier way to get new leads for your business.

I'm not going to lie to you… Having any kind of business isn't easy. You need to stay current, work hard, and focus on the important things. Fortunately, I have a blueprint for helping you to create and maintain a healthy email list which response to your brand in a positive way.

Here's a taste of what you'll learn:

- What Is Email Marketing?
- Different Emails Every Business Should Be Sending
- Email Marketing types: How to Be Different for Each Customer
- Innovate Your Email Marketing: Unlocking the Power of the Fourth Campaign
- How to Set-up Your Sales Funnel
- Email Marketing: 20 Tricks of the Trade
- Conclusion

Starting Today Would You Like to Know More? As you'll see, there are a lot of moving parts in my email marketing system. They all work in a seamless manner. With that said, feel free to pick and choose the techniques you prefer.

My only hope is you'll use this information to make your Email marketing a little more productive. There's a lot to cover.

So let's jump right into it and talk about what email marketing is and the reason you should have email lists of your clients.

WHAT IS EMAIL MARKETING?

You have heard of email marketing repeatedly on the internet, at conferences and during marketing strategy meetings. They say email marketing enriches business communications, targets specific key markets, and is both cost-effective and environmentally friendly. But what exactly is email marketing and how does it work? Or the better question is How will it work for your business? How is an email more effective than a radio spot or television advertisement airing for 30 to 60 seconds every day? And why should a business spending the time to maintain an email list?

Now all these are great questions and by the end of this book we would have answered all of them but first thing first. Why is Email Marketing such a big deal to a business' bottom line? Email marketing is a popular way for businesses to reach customers. According to the Direct Marketing Association, research firms spent over $400 million on direct email marketing alone. Email marketing occurs when your company sends a commercial message to a group of people by use of electronic email. Most commonly use are advertisements, requests for business, or sales or donations, basic any communication sent by email is considered email marketing if the sole purpose is to build customer loyalty, trust in your product or company or brand. Email marketing is a powerful and a very efficient way for your business to stay connected with your clients while also providing a great opportunity and giving you a platform to promoting your business. Who wouldn't love the chance to have access to thousands of customers with the push of a button.

Of course with email marketing you get that chance, where you can easily reach your company's target market without the need for television or radio time or high production costs such as flyers, brochures, posters etc. But thanks to the amazing email marketing software that has been produced over the years, you have the ability to maintain an email list of any size that has been divided up into categories or segments into different sections by common factors like what the customer' likes and dislikes, their spending habits and other important criteria such as birthdays, the day they sign up for the newsletter, whatever way you would like organize the list you can. Then you can create and send out emails which are more laser targeted to the clients on your email list, that way customers are being provided with a personalized email full of detailed information that they are interested in or have personally requested themselves. This is a way that helps to promote trust and form loyalty with your company while also increasing revenue.

There are several examples of email marketing campaigns, one being starting with a welcome email that thanks that new client for opting in to your subscription. Welcome letters are a good way to give valuable information to the customer about your company, plus you can use surveys or call to actions to request important information about your new client. This will give you what you need to put the person in the correct segments for all your future marketing efforts. Now you may be thinking about what are some the things additional email campaigns should include?

Well for starters future email campaigns should include information that will bring brand awareness such as announcements on products or services, or a monthly newsletter regarding your company and/or products, discount coupons for future purchasing, tips and tricks of trade if you are a marketer, but whatever you choose to remember these emails should make the person reading them aware of the benefits your company offers. One thing that should be included in every email you send out should be company information at the bottom after all the content.

Now what this does is give your potential clients a chance to learn more about your company also providing them with the chance to 'opt-in' to get future emails. This is where as well as how you will offer Incentives that give members a 'coupon code' to collect discounts on selected offers, giving you way to monitor the effectiveness of all your campaigns. Also providing information on what your contacts are truly interested in instead sending out emails on topics you think they may like, you can now push content they already like and want to read.

Most companies when it comes to gaining email addresses of their potential customers; they will pay a fee to an email broker, use a subscription service, or just rely on good old fashion referrals from existing customer base. But if you are thinking to yourself well then, which one is good for my business? And the answer would be any and all why? Because most these major companies, use a combination of these methods.

Email marketing is especially popular because it can be much cheaper than traditional email marketing. After all, email does not cost you any postage or printing fees. But it doesn't mean, however, that email is free even though there are some no cost to start options out there.

How does an email marketing campaign incur some fees?

Here is a list of examples...

Your company hires:

- someone to design, write copy for, or oversee the emailing in some way or form,
- Or if you hire a full-time staff member for this type of work, where now the salary or fee of this stall must be paid.
- Or if you choose to purchase the email addresses through an email broker.

One of the great advantages about email marketing is that you have the ability to reach a wide audience in a short period of time. Furthermore, your email marketing campaign can include a number of emails that build upon one another like an email course teaching your clients something they want to learn. One of the most common forms of a building email list is to target a specific upcoming holiday date such as Christmas, Father's Day, or Memorial Day this is where the big businesses make the real money from there bottom line.

If, for example, everyone reading this had to have signed up for Amazon right? Why do you think they ask you for your email when you to sign up? To build up their email list so that when they are planning a large Veterans Day sale, they might send out mass email to their entire list of customers a few weeks in advance announcing the sale, promotion or new product they are launching.

Then the week before send out an additional email as reminder and days before the promotion or product launch they will also be sending out reminders to reinforce the first email. If they didn't have your email what other way could they inform you? May be by phone, now we all know that most of us screen our calls and probably won't pick up the phone or you may just be busy at the time.

With email marketing there's no limits because most people shop and surf from their mobile devices. So now they able to get your message no matter what time you send it out straight into their inbox. Of course it doesn't end but now that you have this ability to get you message into their hands you have to get them to open it, which will cover later further in the book. The whole point about email marketing it gets your message before their eyes where it has the possibility to be seen.

Now email marketing does have its disadvantages like SPAM which an email that is sent out to a huge number of people without any discretion and without any consent from the people receiving the emails. We all have been the victim of the email A-Bomb.

Where you open your inbox and find it full of nothing but junk mail you never content to receive. This is the very reasons, most email services like google, yahoo, AOL include spam filters that weed out this type of emails from your general inbox.

So email marketing is a great weapon to have in your arsenal as a marketing tool. But it has does have to be use with some discretion and with genuine care for your customers.

DIFFERENT EMAILS EVERY BUSINESS SHOULD BE SENDING

Whether you're just starting out with email marketing or you already have some experience sending marketing emails, you've probably wondered about the types of email communication you can send to your database. Should you nurture your subscribers with weekly newsletters?

Are dedicated sends better at optimizing your sales and marketing funnel? What about email digests? These are all valid questions that marketing professionals should consider when selecting the right format to meet their email marketing goals. So which types of emails should you send? In this blog post, we'll discuss the different types of email marketing communication and their respective advantages and disadvantages. This information should help you make both an educated decision when choosing the most appropriate email format to meet your specific goals.

NUMBER ONE: NEWSLETTERS

The first way is you should use the influence of email newsletters in your company's strategy for marketing your business, but before you establish a company newsletter you need to first determine the purpose of it and what you exactly hope to accomplish with the newsletter. Here are a couple of questions you need to ask yourself.

• What is the purpose of your email newsletter?

• What are the goals you hope to achieve with the newsletter?

• How can you nurture your existing customers with your newsletter?

• How is our newsletter make them more aware of your company's brand?

• How can our newsletter inform existing and potential customers of our products and services?

• How our company newsletter going to add value to our customer base?

_____

_____

_____

_____

_____

_____

_____

_____

You may have multiple goals for your newsletter from increasing social sharing of your content, brand awareness, increase sales no matter what your goals are asking yourself, your team these questions will help you achieve those goals your company sets more efficiently. But also while you are going over the metrics of the newsletter always account for how you going to track your newsletter's progress.

Email newsletters can give your business three key advantages. First, they can spread your brand awareness like wildfire, especially if they are shared and go viral. How you say simple: by building consistent communication with your email subscribers, you present them with the opportunity to recognize your brand and associate it with a positive sentiment. Second, email newsletters can help your company leverage existing content, whether from your blog or daily Youtube channel this is a major benefit. Many companies do quick summaries of their most popular blog posts and link to the articles from their newsletter which acts as a traffic enhancer boosting the visitors to that post and truly increasing your company's exposure.

Third, email newsletters give you the freedom to include different kinds of content that might be important to your organization or just beneficial to the customer. Now here is where it gets interesting, say for instance, you want to keep the same newsletter fresh and new you include anything from a popular blog post, a new offer, an announcement of an upcoming event, information about a discount, and a link to a survey the possibilities are endless.

Now like anything there are some disadvantages to Email newsletters. First, they dilute the main call-to-action. Let say you include a series of article summaries, the attention of your recipients will most likely be spread across these tidbits of information as opposed to staying focused on a certain concept. Second, when designing a newsletter things become a more complicated task than other emails like dedicated emails. This is where you'll have to spend some time deciding on the right place of images and text, how they align, and prioritization of the content.

NUMBER TWO, DIGEST

Digests are generally easier to consume than newsletters because they generally consist of links and lists which make the content more readable to your company's email list so they are not overwhelm while reading it. One of the most popular examples of this is the blog digest. What a blog digest does is collects notifications about the articles your company has publish throughout a certain duration of time, then releases an email with the links to that content. If you are blogging and are think of using this option Hub Spot has a great platform, which allows your subscribers to have the opportunity to set up this type of digest based on their likes and dislikes and preferences.

NUMBER THREE, PROMOTIONAL EMAILS

Stand-alone emails also known as Promotional emails, usually focus on containing specific information about just one offer. For instance, you can use a stone-alone email to notify your target audience about a new service you've released or invite them to attend a free event that you're hosting like an online course or webinar.

Promotional emails come with three main advantages. One, they help you to set up a platform to introduce the main call-to-action and which will really drive your results in respect to what you are offering. Two, they are very easy to build. Because once you have your email template in place, building and getting your promotional emails out should be easy. Now of course with newsletters there is a difference, promotional emails don't need to include a lot of the elements we describe earlier to separate the different sections of text and prioritize the content. Three, they are easy to measure.

This is one of the reasons I love promotional emails because they are extremely easy to track. Of course you have to include more than promotional emails in your newsletter, but they are very light -weight in regards to time the consume. Now when you are promoting just one main message along with a call-to-action, it will be easy for you to measure the progress, such as CTR or click-through-rate, your conversion rates, and the leads being generated from the promotional emails.

Like all things as we discuss before Promotional Emails do come with their own disadvantages. One, with promotional emails, the emailing schedule isn't as clear and not as consistent either. You might use promotional emails when you have launched a new offer (which might be sporadic). Now even if you decide to create and maintain a specific schedule for your promotional emails, your subscribers may not realize it or expect communication from you because there is really no clear connection between the separate emails. Two, it's tough to include diverse and fresh content in a promotional email, leaving you with not much room to add other calls-to-actions that might also be important to your company.

NUMBER FOUR: INTRODUCTION SERIES

The Introduction is a tightly connected series of emails full of useful content with a specific purpose such as three or five emails introducing new prospects to the company to brand. In this manner, the Introduction series offers more advantages than just a promotional email being blasted to your subscribers.

Let's take a look at some of the specific advantages the Introduction Series. One, it's timely. Studies show that email response rates decline over the age of the lead, so you need to reach out to your subscribers while they are new, fresh and actively engaged with your brand or company. Two, everything is completely automated. Imagine this once you set up your Introduction series, the emails you have taken the time create just once are sent out automatically according whatever schedule you've set as new leads come in. You are not writing a new email series every time a new prospect signs up for your newsletter they are receiving the same series everybody else got when they subscribe this saves you a boat load time and energy. This leads to a high return on what we call a low cost investment. Three, it is laser-targeted. Now according to the people over at Hub-Spot, lead nurturing emails like these generate an 8% Click-Through-Rates compared to general emails that are sent out, which is said to only generate just a 3% Click-Through-Rates. Simply put targeted and segmented emails perform better than mass emails. Emails also has some disadvantages that you should always keep in mind.

One, the Introduction Series produces less conversation. Promotional emails to your entire subscriber database can generate a lot of conversation around your brand. Introduction series cannot quite achieve the same buzz effect because it is schedule a few emails to a specific audience. Two, it's tracking is more passive. Because Introduction series is automated and are often forgotten about it after they are set it up, it also tends to be under-reported.

NUMBER FIVE: PARTNERSHIP

If you want to expand your reach to a fresh and new audience trying to generate net new leads, you might want to think about trying partnership emails. In partnership emails, you pay for your email inclusion into another online marketer, business, or blogger's newsletter or promotional emails.

Of course one of the biggest advantages of partnership emails is that they are highly targeted; which enables you to be specific in defining the market you want to reach. But it also gives you the opportunity to leverage someone list, without completely exhausting yours. It also allows you to get focus in identifying the different characteristics of your target audience such as; number of employees, geographic location, their interests and challenges, etc. Another advantage of partnership emails is that their ROI or Return On Investment is very easy to figure out. Because you already know how much you are paying the online marketer, you only need to track the results you're generating which are the visits, leads, or sales coming in order to determine what type of return you are getting on the cost you have paid out.

Of course, the disadvantage is that you have to pay for partnership emails. Online marketers, businesses, or bloggers usually will offer different ways for them to receive payments from them allowing you to use their list, and this is where you move into the land of negotiation. Now there's one more disadvantage to partnership emails which is that their management requires a major marketing effort and tight control from the company end. "For this style of partnership to be successful, you need to have set up in your company a dedicated group of people behind it that has an understanding of data, brand synergies, and the ability to unearth unseen co-branding opportunities which will catapult your brands to great heights.

NUMBER FIVE: TRANSACTIONAL EMAILS

Transactional emails are messages that are triggered by a specific action a subscriber may have taken, allowing them to complete that action. For instance, if you are signing up for a FREE webinar to learn 7 things that in the Blogging World, you would fill out a form and then receive a (thank-you) email after the transaction that provides you with the login information in order to join at the time of the webinar. Transactional emails are also the messages you would normally receive from ecommerce sites such as Amazon or E-bay that would confirm the order you just placed and give you the shipment information and other related details.

The biggest advantage of Transactional emails is that they allow you to enjoy those high click-through rates (CTR) we were talking about earlier. Recipients of these types of emails open these communications and click on them. Now if you aren't already you should start taking advantage of this dynamic benefit, and include a highly customized call-to-action tailored to your company such as (maybe as a p.s.) to leverage the fact that the subscriber is fresh and very actively engaged with your emails.

Unfortunately, as all things there is one disadvantage to thank you emails which is that they can add a barrier to action. Sometimes the thought of taking yet another step to complete an action no matter how much they may want it could be discouraging to the recipient and hinder them from completing the action altogether. With all the types of email communications at business' disposal, it's easy to fall into the trap of sending your customers, subscribers too many emails resulting in a burnt out list and you don't want that.

Therefore, it's very important to have some system in place where you can regularly keep track of what messages you're sending and to whom. Now just take a breath, it's entirely possible to send all of these types of emails without becoming a spammer, and that's where segmentation comes into play. A highly productive and effective email marketing campaign should always consist of segmented emails series that touches prospects and leads at the right time with the right type of email to suit that recipient's needs and preferences.

Notes: Take a moment here and write down some of the highlights you would like to work in to your email marketing structure.

_____

_____

_____

_____

_____

_____

EMAIL MARKETING: BE ALL THINGS TO ALL MEN

Now the question I get asked the most is "Are there really different "email marketing types"? Isn't sending an email to a subscriber list just me typing in some content and then hitting the "send" button? Isn't the purpose of email marketing all the same? Absolutely Not! Of course the answer to all questions listed above are "no". Email marketing is, like most marketing pipelines, extremely nuanced and judged based on the different goals that have been set in place, which are accomplished using different strategies. In this Chapter, we'll take a look at the four dimensions of email marketing, what their purpose is, and the basic ways you can start today to implement them.

The best email marketing programs online-to-date integrate mix all four of these dimensions of email marketing. Of course all this is based on where a user or customer is in their customer life cycle may be. After reading this book, you may want to take some time to think about what role email should play in your marketing strategies and which dimension of email marketing will serve both you and your clients best in the long run.

Email Marketing Dimension No. 1. Customer Acquisition and Sales Generating

Now most common type of email marketing used is an email which is constructed with the sole purpose to generate new revenue or increase sales for your company, by either converting your non-existing users or clients to paying customers or by convincing existing customers to make an additional purchase or up sale them to a higher premium offer. Of course, at the end of the day, these four dimensions of email marketing are essentially about creating productive and profitable customers. However, some formats for your emails and other strategies will involve a more direct approach to attempting to generate revenue or sales.

- **Who Receives a Customer Acquisition or Sales Generating Email?** Based on, your user demographic for an email that's been constructed with the sole purpose to generate sales or turn potential users into clients will fall into one of the three categories.

1. The first group will be a list of nothing but potential customers who have never been truly been exposed to your product or service ever before. This where you would mostly would rent or purchase this list from another company and leverage their customer base to grow your company.

2. The second group would be the list of those who have signed up in the past for information about your product or filled out an interest form but have never purchased your service or product.

3. The final group would be of customers who have already purchased from you or visited your website and who may be interested in a follow-up offer this is a great opportunity to up sale them on a premium product or service you want to offer them.

- **What should the Content of a Customer Acquisition or Sales Generating Email Be?**

The content that you include in a sales generating email will be content that will inspire the user to visit your website or make a transaction (such as a CTA or call-to-action). This will typically include some kind of discount or sales offer, but there may be instances where you simply informing them about your product, service or website is good enough.

Sales generating emails will be the backbone of any business hungry to driving direct revenue and get a return-on-investment (ROI) from email marketing. Now however sales generating emails will be more successful when you incorporate them with the other email marketing dimensions we will discussed in the following pages. Because you have to remember that a successful business at is built around the relationships the brand has with their customers. Apple Inc. isn't one of the top four brands used in the world because they just built a good phone, not at all. Steve Jobs was in the business of people. He understood that every time you engage with your customers there is a conversation which based on how things look at the end of this conversation whether or not to trust you or your brand. Or email marketing is a powerful tool because it's one of the most intimate ways to conversation with billions of people from all around the world and build a relationship that will stand the test of time.

Email Marketing Dimension No. 2. Customer Loyalty and Brand Building

Now we touched on this earlier yes, yes, yes I kind of jumped the gun, but I get so excited when we talk about branding and building a business around of the people you serve. One of the greatest books I have read that made this so clear is by an author named Napoleon Hill who wrote "Think, and Grow Rich" which the edited version of the full master class the "The Law of Success" and he gives you this greater understanding that if you get in the habit of giving more then what you expect in return, then you will always get more than you ever gave. Now on that note:

- Have you ever received a newsletter from a blog or company that you've patronized that seemingly had no solicitation for sales or other action on your part?
- What about a thank you email from a company you've done business with that offers you a discount just for having done business with them in the past?

These types of emails are considered customer relational or brand building emails. And simply because the purpose is to keep your brand in the mind of your customers, to have your customers feel like they are building a relationship with you and your company, as a result of doing this, have your customers who stay loyal to using your website, products or services rather than go to a competitor yours.

These emails may not seem like they are bringing in any direct revenue value for you, but the relationship that they're building with your customers and the brand awareness that they're creating means that your customers will remain your customers for longer, spend more of their precious money with you over the long term, and are more likely to become your brand Ambassadors and recommend your brand or company to a friend, family member or colleague. Who can also benefit from your products or services, or just because they love your brand and want others they know to experience it too.

- **Who Should Receive a Brand Building Email?**

  Typically, the best recipients for your brand awareness emails will be your most active clients or your "short-term lapsed" clients those who haven't been engaged in your list for a while. Now I know it can be tempting to create a brand building email and do a mass send to your entire email database very tempting, but emails that generate low open rates or high spam complaints can impact your ability to get your emails into inboxes in the future. So for that reason, you should target customers and users who want to have an ongoing relationship with your brand and build on that loyalty and awareness.

- **What Should the Content of my Brand Building Email Be?**

  The most common type of content found in a brand building email is what you would include in newsletter. Basically providing customers or your users with useful information that is entertaining, engaging, informative and written in the voice of your brand which will cause them to build an affinity for your brand or business. It will also create higher email open and click-through rates(CTRs). Other common brand building emails types include holiday and birthday greetings, thank you emails as we mention earlier, announcements or company status updates, tips and advice emails.

It may seem as though brand building emails do not have an instant return-in-investment (ROI). However, email marketing is one of your most straightforward channels to build a relationship and bridging the gap between your brand and your customers. That relationship, in the long term, can help to grow your business, which increases your revenue and client base.

Email Marketing Dimension No. 3. Customer Retention

Now believe it or not getting customers is the easy part, but now the real question is "How do you keep the customers"? Customer retention in regards to email marketing is any email that takes your existing customers with the purpose to ensure that they remain customers. That they keep coming back to purchase or visit your website again and again. The difference between brand building emails and customer retention emails, they are formatted with prominently the feature of a product or offer. Now, unlike pure sales generating emails which we mention earlier in the book, those offers are typically tailored to appeal just to repeat customers and will likely be less generous in their nature. In essence, this section of your email marketing program is the section that is constructed to maximize the actual revenue or page view value of any previous customer or site user of the brand.

- **Which Customers Should Receive a Customer Retention Email?**

  Simple, any customer who has ever made a purchase from you or registered at your website should be on your customer retention email list. However, ideally you'll segment this list further into types of customers to retain (I talk about list segmentation in my newsletter). But for example, if your business is an electronics store, you may want to send a different customer retention email to customers who have previously purchased phone products than you would to those who have purchased your computer products. The best way to retain customers is to incentivize them or butter the bread as I would say to get them to remain customers by putting the most targeted information and offers as possible in front of them.

- **What Kind of Content Should a Customer Retention Email Contain?**

  Well because a customer retention email is specifically fashioned to spur multiple purchases from a returning customer, the content of this type of email is almost always a promotion or offer, sale, discount or free gift. But however, it is possible to use content that simply makes customers aware of new products (like the launch of a new beauty line) that they may be interested in as a way of keeping them.

Now the most profitable customers are customers in your list who make multiple purchases. People who love your company products and buy anything you are saling just because you're selling. However, there are times when customers need to be reminded that they want to make multiple purchases and this is where you would incentivize them to do so. Just a friendly reminder, all that we have talked about so far to if done, and done right will launch your business out of this stratosphere into levels of growth you never since. But like all things if you don't have a strategic plan for customer retention emails, then you are missing a great part to your email marketing plan.

Email Marketing Dimension No. 4. Customer Win-Back

The final common email marketing dimension is customer win-back email marketing. This is an email which is constructed to "win back" prospects who were once customers or users but have "lapsed" or otherwise fallen away from your product, service, business and brand, to get them back as customers. It is frequently the email marketing scope with the lowest response rate and for this reason should be minimized in how and when it is used, so you don't end up in the long run creating poor email metrics for yourself. However, it is less costly to retain or win back a customer than it would be for you to acquire a new customer. So with that being said, customer win-back emails should always be a part of your email marketing receipt.

- **Who Should Be on My Customer Win-Back Email Campaign?**

  Simply any customer or user who was once a regular purchaser should be on your customer win-back email list, unless they have specifically unsubscribed from emails from your company then you shouldn't worry about them. But, it is often most effective to put them into groups those who are lapsed or abandoned customers based on how long it has been since their last interaction with you and your company. Customers who haven't had a purchasing action in a short amount of time (three months or less) will require a less aggressive offer or sale than customers who have not interacted with you in more than a year or so. By splitting out your email list of inactive customers by time frame, you can create a more impactful email campaign.

- **What Should the Content of Customer Win-Back Email Be?**

  - A customer win-back sale or offer will need to incentivize or (peak the interest of) a customer who has not interacted with you in a very long time to reconnect with to you and your brand. For that reason, these types of marketing emails must include:

    1. **Offers**
    2. **Sales**
    3. **free gifts**

4. free shipping
5. Or other exclusive opportunities that are not available to the general public and that are incredibly compelling to the user.

Your list of inactive customers may be one of the best under used marketing tools in your tool bag as a business, but your response rate here will always be somewhat low. Outside of that email marketing is still the most effective way to attempt to win back customers in your brand or company. Sending an email to a lapsed or inactive customer is incredibly low-cost, so even if you see your response rate is low remember your return on investment (ROI) will be positive.

Now that we've talked about the most common four email marketing dimensions, you may want to take a quick break here to think about and write down below:

How these types of email marketing can work with your brand or marketing goals?

_____

_____

_____

Where in specific should the resources of your business for email marketing campaign go?

_____

_____

_____

_____

When you're done, move on taking some time to think about the various email marketing types as a whole, and you may find your way to have them all in your own email marketing campaign.

THE KING'S BREAD: HOW TO INNOVATE YOUR EMAIL MARKETING CAMPAIGN

Just like with all things in our time there's always room for innovation with your email marketing campaign.

There are those who are quick to write off email as old-fashioned, out-of-date, old man marketing, but let's take a moment and just think about the customer experience. Members of your audience no longer sit down to check their Gmail account once a day, once a week, or once every two weeks; email is very important piece to this new revolution of marketing. The digital world is a very essential and habitual part of the customer experience.

People refresh their email while waiting in line for a pretzel at the mall. Consumers enlist to receive their bills and informal updates via inbox. Social media updates are delivered to the email inbox, with predictions that social is going to eclipse traditional email.

Speaking to a group of marketing executives at Yes Lifecycle Marketing's Innovation Day, Chris Marriott*, vice-president of services and principal consultant at The Relevancy Group, said innovation in email is tied to the customer conversation. Email marketing geared toward driving sales is formulaic, yet the conversation shouldn't stop after a sale. If marketers don't keep their end of the conversation up between purchase cycles, they risk becoming irrelevant or forgotten.

The solution is what Marriott described as a never-ending customer conversation. Here's how to get the conversation started.

Ask the right questions

"Ask questions. Ask what you want the customer to do after he or she has done what you originally wanted them to do," Marriott said. He then compared the ideal marketing campaign to former President Bill Clinton's approach to politics some 20 years ago. As soon as he was elected to the presidency in 1993, he began campaigning for his second term.

"The media dubbed it 'the permanent campaign,'" Marriott said. "Think of your customers as part of your permanent campaign. If you want to keep the dialogue going, what do you do after they've opened, clicked, and completed a purchase? You have to continuously be campaigning and setting the stage for the next purchase." Just think it as a marriage they often say jumping the broom is the easy step, but staying marry now that the hard part. Why because if you were to ask any married couple who understands what it takes to have a long-lasting marriage. They would explain that you are always in a race to keep one another adoration. Same rules apply here you are always race for the customer's adoration.

Embrace the CCCs

Most marketers are so focused on their goal that they've forgotten how to talk to customers, Marriott said. "Buy-now' messaging quickly becomes tired and turns to noise," he said.

Campaign emails can be divided into three major types: content, context, and conversations.

1. **Content emails** are straightforward. They may not be geared toward driving customers toward an immediate purchase, but they provide information (not necessarily related to the brand) that readers might find interesting. An example for a millennial clothing retailer might be a roundup of major music festivals attended by that demographic. Content emails are an easy way to keep the conversation going, so long as they're timed right and they stay relevant.

2. **Context emails** tell consumers why they should care. They're a soft sell for the brand and what differentiates it from competitors. A bakery might share the sorts of ingredients it

uses and how they tie into its philosophy of serving
customers.

3. **Conversations** are key conversation emails make an ask (or
   the ask, if the end goal is a sale). Conversation emails
   mobilize subscribers, asking them to share feedback, share
   photos of them using the product, make a purchase, etc.

Marriott described the "permanent campaign" as a fourth,
underutilized type of email communication.

"Permanent campaign emails fit right into the lifecycle marketing
model," he said. "Most importantly, permanent campaign emails are,
by their nature, perfectly timed when customers may be ready to
purchase again."

Watch for smoke signals

The consumer conversation is a two-way street. Although
marketers should tailor the types of emails they send to their
customers and their stage in the purchase cycle, they should also be
on the lookout for signs that a customer is ready to purchase again.

"In a permanent campaign, businesses can readily and easily
respond to 'smoke signals,' or signs that consumers are about to
purchase again," said Marriott. "Here, data is the key. Unusual

website or social activities are indicators that a customer is ready to purchase and that email communication should be adapted as a result."

Automate

Marriott maintains that at least one-third of emails should be automated based on customer behavior. He described targeting as one of the most underutilized tools despite being a fixture of a permanent campaign.

The Relevancy Group tested welcome campaigns and abandoned shopping cart campaigns for major brands. It found that few are acting on two of the most basic signals that consumers are interested in a brand: offering their email address and placing items in their shopping cart.

To capitalize on the rapport established by content, context, and conversation emails, set up processes to act upon signs that a consumer is close to purchase. If you don't succeed, use that piece of the customer's history to influence future messaging. If items are left in a shopping cart, feature those products in follow-up emails and retargeting programs.

Although continuously communicating with customers, businesses still have an end goal. Don't let the permanent campaign efforts go to waste by failing to act at the appropriate times to achieve these goals.

Consider the Customer perspective

From the customer perspective, all communications coming from your brand should be natural and seamless. If you're engaging in a conversation about mutual interests, they won't be surprised if you eventually make the ask.

Beginning the conversation anew, however, can be jarring. "If a brand contacts me every three months with only an ask, I'm going to wonder why they deserve to be in my inbox even if I've purchased before," Marriott said.

Fundamentally, a never-ending conversation or "permanent campaign" that happens to have a periodic end goal to it. When you incorporate these appropriate types of email communications and automate your reaction to customer signals, your customer won't be caught off guard by a hard sell so long as they "know" the brand.

FAST TRACK: HOW TO SET UP YOUR SALES FUNNEL

*In this final chapter of the **Sales Funnel** we look at how you can begin the process of setting up your own sales funnel based business, whether you have a retail or online business. I will illustrate using an example of the sales funnel I am currently developing for my own online business.*

Find a Profitable Niche

Now that you have realize the potential of a sales funnel and its advantages, which I hope you do by now after reading the previous chapters of this book, you should consider the possibilities of creating one in your niche or market.

A sales funnel can only succeed in a market where there is a demand for what you offer and you are capable of delivering services or products to meet that demand. If you already have an established business, you can always incorporate into business to leverage the products you already created.

What is the niche for your business whether already established or if you are just starting out?

_____

_____

_____

_____

_____

Now assuming you are operating in a marketplace and meet those two criteria we mention earlier, then you have a business and can begin the process of planning your sales funnel.

If you are yet to find your market niche, then your focus must remain on **finding the right business opportunity for you.** Below is a question that can help you find you niche? Now when you ask yourself this question be very honest with yourself. Because you can't build a successful

Sales funnel if you don't have a market for the products and services you sell, so make sure you tick that box first.

What's your passion? What do you love and can easily teach about?

_____

_____

_____

If you are not sure whether you have a good market for a sales funnel you can test by setting up initial lead capture mechanisms and attempt to make front end product sales. This can be as simple as an email newsletter combined with selling an eBook, or even before creating a product, by performing keyword research and setting up a survey site, just like you do with the eBook business model.

Until you have actually made money you can never be certain the potential for a sales funnel based business is there. I'd place more trust in your conversion rate for actual **sales** rather than opt-in rates to a free newsletter as indication of a business opportunity. Having a newsletter as a relationship builder is a great first step – just don't assume people are willing to buy until you sell something.

Planning Your Sales Funnel

Once you are confident you have a profitable niche you can begin work planning your sales funnel.

Your main focus is always **meeting the needs of your customer**. Along the funnel you do this with ever more specifically tailored products. Your ability to charge high ticket prices and make the most profit rests on developing **quality** back end products.

I like to imagine I'm my ideal customer and consider what the core problem is or desire they have that compels them to buy what I offer. If I can help them meet that need then my business will be more successful and I will enjoy immense satisfaction helping others.

It's not always easy to jump into the shoes of your ideal customer, hence the need to gather feedback and survey your prospects and customers. The more focused you can define the problems they face, the better you can tailor the solutions you create.

Initially a need might seem quite broad – say for example "I want to improve my golf game" – but when you dig deeper you might find that it's actually a very specific aspect of the general problem that most people face that you need to focus on, for example "I need to improve my "Putting technique ". Having a "drilled down" understanding of the common problems your customers face when attempting to meet a general need, helps you to determine what products to create.

What is your ideal customer? *Provide as many details about them as possible.*

_____

_____

_____

- How old are they?
- Men or women or both?
- Married or single?
- Parents or not?
- How much education do they typically have? Do they participate in ongoing education as part of their profession? Are there certifications they need?
- Where do they live? Houses, apartments, in the city, in rural area, in the United States, in other countries-which ones?
- How computer savvy are they?
- Do they use high-speed connections? Mobile connections? Surf on their phone?
- What do they do for a living? How much do they earn?
- When do they work on their hobby or business that is your area of expertise?
- How much time and money do they dedicate to your area of expertise?
- Where do they "hang online" Are there forums, member sites, magazine or news sites where you'll find them?

_____

_____

_____

Different Media Communications

Once you have a list of the most common problems in your market you can begin to plan how best to solve them. Consider delivering solutions using different media, such as downloadable audio or video, text, over the phone or in person, conferences, workshops or private tuition.

It's important to remember that different people prefer different methods of learning, and consequently if you can provide solutions using a range of communication methods you stand to help the most people and obtain a larger share of the market.

While it's great to offer many solutions to the most pressing problems your customers face, you also need to consider your ability to deliver. Everyone may prefer private time with you in person, but obviously there is only so much of you to go around. If you are like most entrepreneurs, you are not in the business game to trade time for money, so you probably want to focus on creating methods that do not require your personal attention to deliver.

Digital Goodies

A common practice at the **front end** of a sales funnel for an online business is to focus on digital goods. Goods that will give the customer or subscriber instant gratification such as: eBooks, reports, recorded audio, transcripts, Screen-O-matic video presentations and other products that can be delivered via the web can satisfy many hundreds or even thousands or millions of customers without you having to work any harder with each new purchase. You create the product once and assuming it remains current, it is set-and-forgotten.

As you move down the funnel you can still use digital products to satisfy your **hyper-responsive** customers, perhaps with more highly tailored content (an even more refined problem), or by delivering your most advanced techniques or offering a larger package of Course you may have create of the topic, bundles of products.

Generally, as customers move towards your **back end**, especially if you operate an information publishing business based on your expertise, they expect to receive more personalized attention. The back end is often where private coaching or small workshops work well. You can gather a very small group of your overall customer base, who are prepared to pay a premium price and travel to come work with you in a more intimate format.

- **What are some the digital goodies here you could create for your front end?**

_____

_____

_____

- Now off the ideas you have for front-end how can you take it to next level like courses, trainings, webinars, seminars etc.?

_____

_____

_____

Perception and the Offer

It's important to realize that although you might have assumptions of what people expect for their money and how much they are willing to pay, both in the front and back ends, the primary drivers are actually **perceived value** and the **offer** you present. What the actual product is and how you deliver it do not factor in as much as you might think.

There has to be some correlation between how much you charge and the type of product people receive for their money, it's actually more important **how you market your offer** than anything else.

There's a common perception of marketers that they cheat and lie in order to make sales – and some do – but I think it's important to distinguish between a constructed offer and misleading the market, before applying the label of "evil marketer". The line between an emotionally compelling offer and misleading people with hype can be a fine one at times, and I'm not writing this book to debate the ethics of marketing, but it's a point worth making.

A good offer is a preposition that a certain product or service will meet a specific need. What makes the offer compelling is how the marketing materials tap all the right triggers (social proof, empathy) in the people who possess the need and how well refined the problem is. With that level of clarity, it is possible to create a **perception** that you offer the best solution and can charge a **premium price**. Whether you actually present the best solution is a moot point – there really is no such thing as a "best solution" – it's all about how people feel and what they perceive as the best solution.

How can you preposition your Offers to be perceive by your audience (social proof or empathy)?

_____

_____

_____

Beginner Sales Funnel Building

I expect many of you reading this are like me, independent, small business owners, who produce products and services mostly by yourself. You might outsource certain tasks, but product and content creation is your responsibility. You have a topic area that you love and blog about, or run a business in an industry you know reasonably well. Your interest in creating a sales funnel is high because you can see the potential, but you have to realize certain resource limitations hold you back from creating a super-sized, uber-sales funnel quickly.

For many people who operate online businesses they never go past the front end. They might have an email newsletter, or a free e-course, or a website or blog as a lead generator and then sell entry level products like books, or software, or templates or videos, but that's as far as they go down the rabbit hole still not taking full advantage of the little red pill. The same goes for **affiliate marketers**, or **AdSense earners** – you may make good money from it but it's all about one-off front end sales or clicks.

The Big Picture Mindset

To start building your sales funnel you need to **think beyond that first sale** and see the **big picture**. Questions you need to ask yourself:

- Are the people who buy your book or eBook coming back with questions?
- Can you take those questions (problems) and make more products?
- Do they love what you do that they will lap up everything you produce?
- Are you building an email list and segmenting it into different customer groups so you can create different products?
- Do you have plans for up-sells and cross-sells?

- Can you see yourself creating a large, home-study package selling for $297 with a big product launch that makes five figures like the guru Internet marketers do?

All these different aspects can be part of your sales funnel but the most important concept to grasp is that your first product or your current email newsletter or blog are just front end components or what we call in the business world the "Tripwire", and if you one day want a thriving business turning over six or seven figures, in most cases **developing a back end of products that you will be able to up sale to is the way to go**. Take a moment now and think about write down what comes to you as you ask yourself these questions:

_____

_____

_____

_____

_____

_____

_____

Nothing Set in Stone

One thing to accept is that the process of building a sales funnel is not set in stone. You do want to create a reasonably consistent back end, but the process of developing one takes testing and effort. You have to consider what products to offer, produce the products, what offers to present to the market and test all the metrics that make up the system. This is a significant job, something you can't do over night and you will probably need to bring in specialized talent to handle some of the areas, especially if metrics and testing are not your strong point. But overall once you have the foundation set you are pretty much good to go.

Thank you

Now my hope is that this book has in some way help and truly given you a clear understanding of Email Marketing, plus why it should be part of your marketing strategies. I do appreciate you stay with all the way till end; I have been told by my wife that I could be a little long winded about things I am passionate about. But before you go, I'd like to say "thank you" for purchasing my eBook. I know you could have picked from dozens of books on email marketing. But you took a chance with my guide. So a big thanks for downloading this book and reading all the way to the end. So as a token of my appreciation for letting me talk your ear off and as a way of saying thanks for purchasing this book, I'm offering you a copy of my next book for free that's exclusive to my readers. Just head over to www.richardallenwilliamsjr.com and sign up to receive a notice when it is released so can grab your free copy. If you liked this book, then I need your help. Please take a moment to leave a review for this book on Amazon. This feedback will help me continue to write the kind of Kindle books that helps you get results. And if you love it, then please let me know :-)

CONCLUSION

In conclusion, if you are considering an email marketing campaign, make sure that your practices are in keeping with spam laws. Adult content spam, for example, has been addressed by legislation under the United States' CAN-SPAM Act (Controlling the Assault of Non-Solicited Pornography and Marketing Act). Furthermore, if the administrator of your Internet service believes that you might be sending spam; your emailing service might be temporarily shut down. Please take a note.

www.ingramcontent.com/pod-product-compliance
Lightning Source LLC
Chambersburg PA
CBHW071827200526
45169CB00018B/1105